THE COMPETITION BICYCLE
A PHOTOGRAPHIC HISTORY

Jan Heine
Photographs by Jean-Pierre Pradères

VINTAGE BICYCLE PRESS
SEATTLE

INDEX

Throughout this book, chapter headings include the riders of the bikes shown, for example, the actual bike which Fausto Coppi rode to victory in the 1949 Tour de France, on page 88. Where no rider name is listed, we do not know who rode the bike. The dates on this page refer to the events described in the corresponding chapters. The specifications on page 170 list the dates when each bike was built.

CYCLES BARRET
1880–1885

page **6**

HUMBER
1894/95

page **12**

DURSLEY PEDERSEN RACER
1903

page **18**

LABOR TOUR DE FRANCE
1910

page **24**

AUTOMOTO TOUR DE FRANCE
1926

page **28**

ALCYON TOUR DE FRANCE
1927

page **34**

BASTIDE STAYER
1920s

page **40**

WILLY APPELHANS SIX-DAY
Frank Bartell
1935
page **46**

JOE KOPSKY
Doris Kopsky
1937
page **50**

OSCAR EGG
1939

page **54**

CAMINARGENT BORDEAUX-PARIS
Ca. 1939

page **60**

DELANGLE TANDEM
Maurice Richard / Dayen
1936
page **66**

DELANGLE TRACK
1939

page **70**

BARRALUMIN
René Vietto
1948
page **72**

WILIER TRIESTINA
Fiorenzo Magni
1948
page **78**

BARTALI
Gino Bartali
1949
page **82**

BIANCHI
Fausto Coppi
1949
page **88**

RENÉ HERSE
CRITERIUM DES PORTEURS
1950s
page **94**

BIANCO ROAD
Georges Baudin
1950s
page **98**

BIANCO TRACK
Georges Baudin
1950s
page **102**

BASTIDE STAYER
Georges Baudin
1950s
page **104**

ROCHET SUPER SPECIAL
1950s
page **106**

RENÉ HERSE TANDEM
Lucien Détée / Gilbert Bulté
1956
page **110**

CINELLI SUPERCORSA
Bruce Waddell
1965
page **118**

RENÉ HERSE COURSE
Geneviève Gambillon
1972
page **122**

EDDY MERCKX/DE ROSA
Eddy Merckx
1974
page **126**

J. P. WEIGLE
Peter Weigle
1975
page **132**

GITANE
Greg LeMond
1981
page **136**

MIKE MELTON/HUFFY
John Marino
1982
page **140**

CUNNINGHAM
Jacquie Phelan
1983
page **146**

MOSER
Francesco Moser
1984
page **152**

LANDSHARK/HUFFY
Andy Hampsten
1988
page **156**

CONCORDE
Sean Kelly
1991
page **160**

COLNAGO
Tony Rominger
1994
page **164**

Preface

Bicycles are the most efficient machines, allowing their riders to go faster and further than otherwise possible by human power alone. Perhaps due to this efficiency, bicycles always have inspired competition.

As soon as children learn to balance on two wheels, they challenge each other to race down the block, up the hill, and beyond. Even the most serene cyclotourist's pace quickens imperceptibly when they see another rider on the horizon. Many cyclists partake in organized competition in one form or another.

Competition on bicycles can take many forms. Great champions battle the mountain passes of the great tours. Others whirl around the banked oval of a track. Randonneurs embrace the open road unsupported. Newspaper carriers raced each other over the cobblestones of Paris with 15 kg of newspapers on the front rack. Mountain bikers do away with roads altogether and race on mountain trails.

Each of the bikes in the following pages was hand-crafted by a master builder for the rigors of its specific event. As road conditions and race tactics changed over time, so did the bicycles that carried their riders to victory. The bicycles in this book chart the development of competition bicycles from Racing High Wheelers to modern bikes that fought for the most prestigious of all cycling awards, the hour record. Each bike highlights a chapter in the history of the competition bicycle.

As far as possible, I have selected original machines with competition histories, which tell their stories through sweat-stained handlebar tape and well-worn saddles. These are the actual bikes on which great champions and other competitors surged toward the finish line.

—*Jan Heine*

Eddy Planckaert (left) outsprints Guido Van Calster (center) and Bernard ▶
Hinault (right) to win stage 12b of the 1981 Tour de France in Zolder, Belgium.
(Photo: John Pierce, Photosport International)

THE FIRST RACING MACHINES

Almost as soon as the Freiherr Baron von Drais invented the hobby horse in 1817, riders challenged each other to see who could go faster. The first global bicycle boom of the 1860s also saw the first organized bicycle races, where riders on boneshakers with wooden wheels and iron rims competed against each other. Thousands of spectators came to see the new machines battle each other, or even be matched against horse-mounted riders.

Early bicycles had a direct drive to the front wheel. Increasing the size of the wheel increased the gearing and thus allowed riders to go faster. Thus the "High Wheeler" or "Ordinary" was invented, but the inseam of the rider, who had to straddle the front wheel, limited the wheel size and therefore the bike's top speed. Even a tall machine like the one shown here, with a huge 140 cm (55") front wheel, required the rider to spin at 121 revolutions per minute to achieve a speed of 32 km/h (20 mph).

▲ Cycle track race in Chicago around 1889.
(Photo: Lorne Shields Bicycle Collection)

Unable to increase the gearing further, makers began to look elsewhere for speed. Riders quickly realized that light weight brought faster acceleration and less resistance. Brakes, lamps and other accessories were deleted from the racing machines.

During the 1870s and 1880s, progress was incredibly swift. Only 15 years earlier, boneshakers had used wooden wheels and iron frames, yet the racing machine shown here is equipped with a tubular backbone (frame) and tubular fork blades, which greatly reduce its weight. The steerer also is tubular, and an open head tube saves further weight. The entire bicycle weighs just 11.7 kg (25.7 lbs.), at a time when most touring machines weighed twice as much. To improve the strength of the front wheel, the hubs are machined with extra-wide flange spacing (133 mm), and the spokes are crossed, as well as tied and soldered. The pedals and front hub are equipped with ball bearings, while the headset turns in conical sleeve bearings.

The head tube of this wonderfully preserved machine reads "Cycles Barret, Champion de France," but the details of this maker and their championship win have been lost in the mist of time.

High Wheel racer ▶
(Photo: E. M. Middleton, Aberdeen, Scotland; Lorne Shields Bicycle Collection)

▼ The solid rubber tires that used to cover the 16-mm-wide rims are missing from this otherwise all-original racing High Wheeler.

The First Long-Distance Road Races

The tall stature and great cost of High Wheelers appealed to dashing, well-off sportsmen. Like horses, the High Wheelers were used for parading around town, and many bicycle races were held on horse-racing tracks.

In the late 1880s, a new type of bicycle took the world by storm. The "Safety" used a chain to drive the rear wheel. The name emphasized the relative safety of the new machines. Its riders no longer feared the dangerous "headers," which had been common on High Wheelers, where the rider perched precariously on top of the giant front wheel. The "Safety" had another advantage: Its gearing depended not on the size of the driven wheel, but on the ratio of the cogs in the transmission. The Humber shown here is relatively low-geared (18 x 8), yet the bicycle travels slightly further with each pedal revolution than the High Wheeler shown in the previous chapter. The "Safety" enabled riders to venture farther, and soon long-distance races on the open road became more common. Pneumatic tires brought a further increase in speed and comfort.

Bicycle racer ▶
(Photo: Lorne Shields Bicycle Collection)

HUMBER

The early long-distance races were true adventures. Riders used pacers on bicycles to break the wind, unlike today, where outside help is not permitted. When the pacers were exhausted, they dropped back, but often, their replacements were not at the assigned spots. Then the racer had to continue alone. The roads often were mere paths, and riders sometimes carried pistols to ward off dogs or highway robbers. When their fragile pneumatic tires punctured, racers relied on mechanics from the tire manufacturers, who performed the difficult and time-consuming repairs. The mechanics traveled by train to the towns along the course, waiting for the racers in case repairs were needed.

Also traveling by train between checkpoints were newspaper reporters, who telegraphed stories about the racers' exploits to their editors. These heroic races captured the imagination of the public, and the first veritable bicycle boom started when mass production brought the price of bicycles within reach of many.

The first "Safeties" had ungainly "x-shaped" or "open" frames, but it took only a few years until the modern "diamond" frame was adopted almost universally as the most logical solution. This Humber was built in 1984 or 1895 as a top-of-the-line racing machine, equipped with a lugged frame brazed from lightweight steel tubing. The rear hub features outboard bearings and zero dish to increase the spokes' lifespan. The cloth-covered wooden rims carry 43 mm wide clincher tires. At a time when tires were custom-made to order, there was no need to standardize wheel sizes, so the Humber's front wheel is bigger than the rear one. The bracket on the headset can hold a lamp for night-time riding.

The entire bicycle weighs just 12.5 kg (27.5 lbs.). It has survived almost unridden in completely original condition. Even though its original tires no longer hold air, we still can imagine the sense of freedom that this machine inspired in its riders, as they spun their fixed gear over hill and dale on the finest British ball bearings and wide pneumatic tires.

A Novel Approach to Comfort and Speed

Even though the modern shape of the bicycle was well-established by the mid-1890s, not everybody was satisfied with the standard machines. Especially the saddles caused much discomfort, and even today, saddle makers continue to introduce new models and new ideas with the goal of making cycling more comfortable.

Mikael Pedersen, a Danish inventor living in Dursley, England, developed a woven bicycle seat that was not mounted on a firm post, but suspended like a hammock. Mounting such a saddle on a standard bicycle frame was difficult, so he invented a bike to go with his saddle. The result was one of the most radical departures from the traditional "diamond" frame. Sold as the Dursley Pedersen, this machine had a triangulated frame made from small-diameter tubing. The saddle was suspended between the head joint and two cantilevered tubes at the rear of the bicycle. The rider's weight was balanced with tension rods, which connected the rear of the saddle to the rear dropouts. The fork consisted of four tubes and was supported in two locations. The resulting frame was among the lightest available at the time. The handlebars were attached to the middle of the fork, where they could be connected to all four fork tubes. This greatly reduced the flex in the steering that occurs with a standard stem and handlebar combination.

As with most deviations from standard diamond frames, the Pedersen is not without critics. However, the frame is triangulated both vertically, to support the rider's weight, and laterally, to resist flexing when pedaling. You cannot help but be intrigued by these completely different machines, especially since they ride remarkably well. In their time, they were quite successful, with more than 7000 built over a 15-year period.

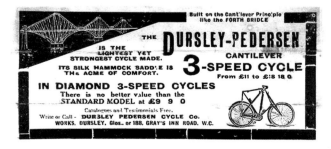

◀ Pedersen drew on the principles of bridge design in his frame construction.
(Advert courtesy David Evans)

While most Dursley Pedersens were used for touring, often with a novel 3-speed hub with internal gears, a few superlight racing models were built and ridden in races and record attempts. Harry "Goss" Green was a famous recordman at the turn of the 20th century. Riding for the Silverdale Cycling Club on a Dursley-Pedersen, "Goss" Green did not just eke out new records by a few minutes, but completely smashed the existing records. Many of his records stood for decades. In October 1900, "Goss" Green completed the 197.5 miles from London to York in 11:19 hours behind a motorpacer, improving upon the previous record by almost two hours. Green's record stood for 26 years. Performances like these brought welcome publicity to the Dursley Pedersens.

This ultra-rare racing Dursley Pedersen dates from around 1903. Its weight of only 9.8 kg (21.5 lb.) confirms the period advertising claims of superlight weight, especially since the bike now is equipped with heavy and probably not original steel rims. Today, several makers offer replicas of touring Dursley Pedersens, but nobody has cloned the superlight racing machines yet.

The Most Rigid and Solid of All Bicycles?

In 1910, the standard diamond-frame bicycle was barely 20 years old, yet all racing bicycles already resembled each other. Rather than fine-tune the diamond frame's performance, the French bicycle manufacturer Labor proposed a radically new frame design for their "Tour de France" model.

Instead of supporting each wheel on both sides, the "Tour de France" used single-sided attachments for front and rear wheels. Apart from its radical looks, this allowed changing tires without removing the wheel. To counter concerns about a lack of stiffness, Labor doubled up the right chainstays and attached an additional stay to the center of the seat tube, for a total of four stays.

A curved tube under the top tube was intended to add more strength, similar to the arch of a bridge. Labor conveniently overlooked that unlike bridges, top tubes are not loaded in the center of the span. Instead of a slotted rear dropout, the "Tour de France" used an eccentric bottom bracket to tension the chain.

At 13 kg (28.6 lbs.), the "Tour de France" weighed no more than conventional racing bikes of its era. Its high price of 300 Francs – 40 Francs more than Labor's conventional "Special Course" model – probably explains why the unconventional design was not very popular. Perhaps cyclists also felt that removing the wheel from the bike was preferable to handling the entire bicycle when mounting a tire. All this did not prevent Cannondale from re-introducing single-bladed forks on their mountain bikes in the 1990s.

The Labor headbadge shows how the bike's top tube configuration ▶ was inspired by a railroad bridge.

26

Giants of the Road

By the 1920s, the Tour de France had become the battleground of trade teams that raced in the colors of large bicycle and tire manufacturers. The two most powerful teams were Automoto-Hutchinson and Alcyon-Dunlop. The 1926 Tour de France was the longest of all Tours to date, with 5745 km divided into just 17 stages. That year's shortest stage was 275 km long – longer than the longest stage of the 2008 Tour. One stage was particularly challenging. The 323 km "Circle of Death" from Bayonne to Luchon crossed six large cols: Osquich, Aubisque, Soulor, Tourmalet, Aspin and Peyresourde. Seventy-six riders left Bayonne at midnight, and it was almost dinner time when the first rider, Lucien Buysse, struggled into Luchon after more than 17 hours in the saddle. The next rider arrived many minutes later, and 22 riders abandoned the race during this stage. On this day, Lucien Buysse won the Tour de France, because he kept his lead to the end. It was not an exciting race. The yellow jersey changed hands only twice during the entire Tour de France, and the deciding stage's average speed of just 19 km/h (12 mph) was nothing to write home about.

Tour organizer Henri Desgrange blamed the large teams for the lack of drama in the Tour, and he was determined to change this. For the 1927 Tour, 16 of the 24 stages were run as team time trials. This meant that racers did not know where their competitors were. They had to ride all-out instead of taking it easy as the pack made its way around France, waiting for the mountains to decide the race. While Desgranges achieved his goal of increased speed, roadside spectators got confused when they saw the yellow jersey pass far behind other riders, whose teams had started earlier. To top it off, the winner, Nicolas Frantz, rode for Alcyon, one of the big teams whose grip on the Tour Desgrange wanted to break.

Most racers used a fixed cog (16 teeth; left side) for flat roads and ▶ a single-speed freewheel (20 teeth; right) for climbing and descending. To change gears, the racer removed the rear wheel and turned it around before re-installing it. Hubs and bottom bracket of this top-of-the-line 1926 Automoto were equipped with oiler holes.

Nicolas Frantz repeated his win in 1928, when he became the first rider to wear the yellow jersey during every single stage. At least this race saw some excitement during stage 19. Frantz had a lead of more than an hour going into the stage, but the frame of his bike broke. Frantz continued the stage on a woman's bike, which he borrowed from a bike shop owner or a spectator, depending on which version of the story you believe. Over the remaining 100 km, he lost half an hour to the stage winner, but his lead remained safe.

In the end, Desgrange may have had himself to blame for the slow pace of his Tours de France. With stages that took more than 10 hours of riding on poor roads, crashes and equipment failures determined the outcome almost as often as athletic ability. In the mountains, the peloton rarely stayed together, and riders trickled in one by one. It was a heroic sport, but not a media-friendly one.

▲ Lucien Buysse on the Col d'Aubisque during the stage that won him the 1926 Tour de France. Buysse rode for Automoto.
(Engraving: Miroir Archives – Photosport International)

◀ The 1926 Automoto "Tour de France" was the top-of-the-line model.

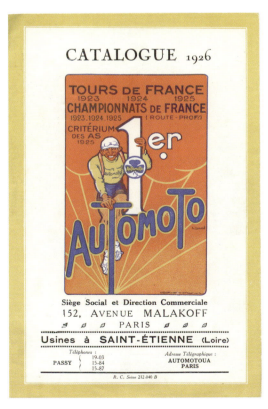

AUTOMOTO

Both the 1926 Automoto and the 1927 Alcyon shown on these pages are top-of-the-line "Tour de France" models. They are similar to the bikes ridden by the great champions, yet they are not light at 12.5 and 13.0 kg (27.5 and 28.6 lb.), respectively. The unpaved mountain passes of the Tour de France required rugged bicycles and discouraged experimentation. Throughout the 1920s, bicycle technology stagnated as the brightest engineers turned their skills to motorcars and airplanes. Durability and ease of maintenance were more important than light weight and ease of changing gears. Equipped with a freewheel on one side of the rear hub for mountain stages and a fixed gear on the other side for flat stages, shifting gears required removing the rear wheel and installing it reversed.

As long as all racers were doing this, it did not make a difference in race tactics. Derailleurs already were used by cyclotourists, but they did not work well in mud and thus were poorly suited for racing. In any case, Tour organizer Henri Desgrange believed that real men did not use these new-fangled devices. The Tour de France was his race, so he simply prohibited his professional racers from using derailleurs. To break the power of the commercial teams, Desgrange had another trick up his sleeve. Starting in 1930, he simply abolished the commercial teams altogether and ran the Tour for national teams instead.

▲ The Automoto's frame was made from thick-walled steel tubes, which were brazed into straight-cut lugs.

◄ The Bowden "Touriste" brake attached not to the seatstay bridge, but was clamped to the stays themselves. Brake blocks and tires are original from 1926.

33

1926 Automoto

1927 Alcyon

▲ Using a fitting on the seatpost, a reservoir in the seat tube can be filled with oil. When the oiler is tipped down, oil drips onto the chain.

The Alcyon's frame is gas-welded from steel tubing. ▲

Nicolas Frantz on the Col d'Aubisque during his winning ride in the 1928 Tour de France. Frantz rode for Alcyon.
(Photo: Miroir Archives – Photosport International)

Motor-Paced Stayer

From the early beginnings of "Boneshakers" on horseracing tracks, track racing evolved into two different directions. In short events, sprinters displayed pure speed, as well as tactics and skill. In distance events, riders needed extraordinary stamina over several hours or even days. To enliven the spectacle of the distance races, organizers encouraged pacing, first by other cyclists, then tandems, quads and quints, and finally motorcycles. These "stayer" races were popular, since they combined the familiar bicycle with the motorized symbols of progress. Spectators got a glimpse into the world of rich people, a world that was closed to the majority of the population. At a time when progress meant speed, the thundering machines traveled at incredible velocities of more than 100 km/h (60 mph), and records were broken on a regular basis.

◀ German champion Walter Sawall and an unidentified rider at a stayer race in Berlin, 1929.
(Photo: Express Photo Centrale Berlin, Jeff Groman Collection)

Stayers ride at higher speeds than other cyclists, making theirs a most dangerous occupation. They require strong and reliable frames, and many champions turned to E. Bastide in Paris for suitable machines.

Starting before 1913, Bastide's frames featured many novel ideas that since have become commonplace. He was among the first to use straight, round chainstays, rather than stays that curved in an S-bend around the rear tire. He also brazed the seatstays to the seat lug and dropouts, rather than bolting them in place. All these features made Bastide's frames stronger and stiffer than the old-fashioned frames.

Even today, stayer frames still follow the design of the early machines. To receive a better draft, the cyclist has to follow the motorpacer as closely as possible. A small front wheel and a fork with reversed rake allow closer drafting. A forward-mounted saddle and an extra-long stem further move the cyclist's body forward.

Bastide stayer bikes remained popular for many years after Bastide closed his shop in 1936. This machine dates from the 1920s, but was updated with new wheels and possibly a new stem in the late 1940s. For more than 20 years, it followed the roaring motorbikes around the track at dizzying speeds.

Motorpaced World Record
Frank Bartell

While Europeans enjoyed motorpaced stayer races, American spectators loved Six-Day races more than any other sport. Each Six-Day team consisted of two racers. One team member rested while the other raced around the track. Races went non-stop for six days and six nights.

During the "Roaring 20s," huge crowds packed the halls where the races were held on specially constructed board tracks. Intermediate sprints provided extra points, which counted toward the final score. The atmosphere reached a fever pitch when celebrities enlivened the race by offering cash bonuses, or "primes," for the next sprint. Old-timers still talk of the nights when actress Peggy Hopkins Joyce offered one $ 1000 prime after another, while the band played "Pretty Peggy with Eyes of Blue." Crashes further added to the spectacle: One poster advertised "Thrills and Spills." Gossip newspapers reported on the private lives of the stars and their ordeals on the track. It was show business at its very best.

The "Roaring 20s" were followed by the Great Depression of the 1930s. Fewer people could afford to attend sports events. To lure visitors to the Six-Day races, promoters had to think of unusual ideas. Before the 1935 Los Angeles Six-Day Race, the organizers had star rider Frank Bartell pace behind the fastest car in Hollywood, a souped-up Auburn owned by cowboy film star Tom Mix. Bartell got up to 80.5 mph (128.8 km/h) for a minute on Lincoln Boulevard, setting a world record for paced speed on the road. Reports of the record ride in the local papers helped draw spectators to the races.

▲ Frank Bartell on one of his Six-Day machines.
(Photo: Jeff Groman Collection)

Bartell's bike is a standard Six-Day racer. It was built by Willy Appelhans, whose shop in the Bronx (New York) specialized in Six-Day machines. Its sturdy construction resembles that of the 1920s Tour de France machines. Even so, the top tube has numerous dents that remind of crashes on the tracks.

At 12 kg (26.5 lbs.), Bartell's bike is not light, especially for a track racing machine. For his record ride, Bartell used a huge custom-machined chainring, but otherwise, his bicycle remained a standard Six-Day racer. This was the last time that the motorpaced record was broken on a standard track bike, rather than a machine built specifically for the record attempt.

▲ Frank Bartell set a motorpaced record of 80.5 mph in 1935.
(Photo: Jeff Groman Collection)

WOMEN'S NATIONAL CHAMPION
Doris Kopsky

During the 1860s, women's bicycle races were popular, not so much as sporting events, but more for their scandalous novelty. As cycling became mainstream, women were banned from racing in accordance with the mores of the time. However, women continued to ride, and bicycles gave them independence that contributed to their emancipation. Before long, women demanded and obtained equal rights to men in politics, society and sports. And with that, they began to race bicycles again. In 1937, the Amateur Bicycle Association (ABA) organized the first "girls' division" championships in Buffalo, New York. The "girls" were women of any age.

At the inaugural event, it was indeed a girl who won. Fifteen-year-old Doris Kopsky raced one mile on the dirt track in 4 minutes and 22.4 seconds, beating the other competitors. Doris came from a family of bicycle racers. Her father, Joseph (Joe) Kopsky, was a steelworker, who worked on the skyscrapers that made Manhattan's skyline world-famous during the 1910s and 1920s. He was a strong cyclist and had been part of the U.S. cycling team at the 1912 Olympic games in Stockholm. That year, the U.S. team won a bronze medal, the last Olympic medal won by a U.S. cyclist for 72 years.

▲ Doris Kopsky after the 1937 National Championships, flanked by Furman Kugler (Junior Champion) on the left and Charles Bergna (Senior Champion) on the right.
(Photo: Jeff Groman Collection)

Joe Kopsky built Doris' bike based on his own ideas. It is leagues ahead of the relatively crude Six-Day machines common in the U.S. at the time. The lugs are nicely filed and thinned. The geometry was custom-designed for Doris' physique. Hubs and bottom bracket used cartridge bearings. Joe Kopski patented these components in 1931, making them among the earliest bicycle components with modern cartridge bearings.

Doris used her bike well. She won numerous Eastern and National dirt track titles and roller races from 1936 to 1941. She also was the New Jersey State Sprint Champion in 1937, 1938 and 1939. However, it took decades for women's racing to become truly accepted. A small step along the way occurred in 1954, when the ABA changed the title from "girls' championship" to "women's championship."

Derailleurs on Racing Bikes

The ability to change a bicycle's gear ratio on the fly had existed since the late 19th century. The early designs used twin chains, chains running in figure-8 configurations, and internally-geared hubs. However, racers had resisted these adventurous contraptions, both because they were afraid of added friction, and because the shifting devices could be unreliable during the long stages and on the poor roads of the time. By the early 1930s, most racers had adopted three-speed freewheels, but still had to stop the bike and move the chain by hand, and then re-tension the chain after they had completed the gear change.

To overcome the racers' skepticism, former racer and hour record holder Oscar Egg designed a racing-specific derailleur. His revolutionary "Super Champion" was introduced in 1934. A spring-loaded arm underneath the bottom bracket tensioned the chain, and thus eliminated the need to reposition the rear wheel after each shift. A simple shifter fork in front of the rear wheel moved the chain from one cog to the next. During normal operation, only the roller of the tensioner touched the chain. Unlike touring derailleurs with their multiple bends of the chain, the chain run was close to that of a single-speed bicycle, which was thought to reduce friction.

Knowing that few racers would give his derailleur a lengthy trial, Egg designed an indexing shift lever that made shifting fool-proof. The derailleur worked well and was easy to retrofit on most racing bikes.

▲ Derailleurs had been admitted to the Tour de France only a year before Gino Bartali climbed the Izoard on his way to win the 1938 Tour. Bartali used the Italian Vittoria Margherita derailleur with shifter paddles above the chainstay, requiring him to backpedal while changing gear. The rider behind Bartali used a Super Champion derailleur.
(Photo: Miroir Archives – Photosport International)

Racers were very concerned with a straight chainline. ▶
With a three-speed freewheel, the chain ran almost straight in every gear. For flat courses, a fourth, smaller, fixed cog was mounted on the left side of the rear hub. To use it, the racer had to stop and turn around the rear wheel.

Racers quickly adopted the Super Champion, and it was found on most French racing bikes of the late 1930s. In 1937, the Tour de France organizers finally allowed racers to use derailleurs, and standardized the Super Champion for all participants. (Only the Italian team was allowed to use the similar Vittoria Margherita.) The result was a great increase in speed: The last rider completed the race at a faster average speed than the previous year's winner.

In addition to derailleurs, Oscar Egg sold complete bicycles in his shop at Avenue de la Grande Armée in Paris, not far from the Arc de Triomphe. The bike shown here was a top-of-the-line racing bike. The frame is made from lightweight butted steel tubing. Aluminum is used for rims, brakes, handlebars, stem and numerous other parts. The geometry resembles that of a modern racing bike. The entire bike weighs just 9.9 kg (22 lbs.). Machines like these were a huge step forward from the heavy bikes of the 1920s. The amateur racer who owned this bike could be proud of his machine.

The Super Champion features an indexing shift lever. ▶ The rider has to pull the lever outward and shift two notches to move the chain, then shift back one notch to center the shifting fork on the chain. The backing plate has two stops that allow moving the shift lever beyond the three indexing holes. The indexing feature makes shifting with the Super Champion easy and foolproof.

Airplane Technology

Aluminum had been known for centuries, but in its raw form, it lacked strength for use in engineering applications. The 1920s saw great technological advances in materials and technology, when various aluminum alloys were developed that combined strength with light weight. The first airplane flights across the Atlantic Ocean, the Zeppelin airships that were lighter than air, racing cars with aluminum engines and wheels – all became possible with the modern alloys. Within a decade, this new technology found use on bicycles as well.

Pierre Caminade was at the forefront of these developments. He introduced aluminum stems and handlebars in the 1920s, and then expanded into rims and saddles with undercarriages made from aluminum alloys. In 1936, Caminade began producing his Caminargent racing bikes. The frames were made from extruded octagonal tubing, which was bolted together in cast aluminum lugs. This top-of-the-line racing model is equipped with the rare and expensive Stronglight aluminum cranks, as well as aluminum rims, stem and handlebars made by Caminargent. The Idéale saddle has an aluminum undercarriage. The resulting bike weighs just 9.0 kg (19.8 lbs.).

The ends of the tubes were filled with cork, which was said to improve shock absorption. The corks in the fork blades are visible at the top of the fork crown. Originally, the bike ran on smooth tires, rather than the cyclocross tires now mounted.

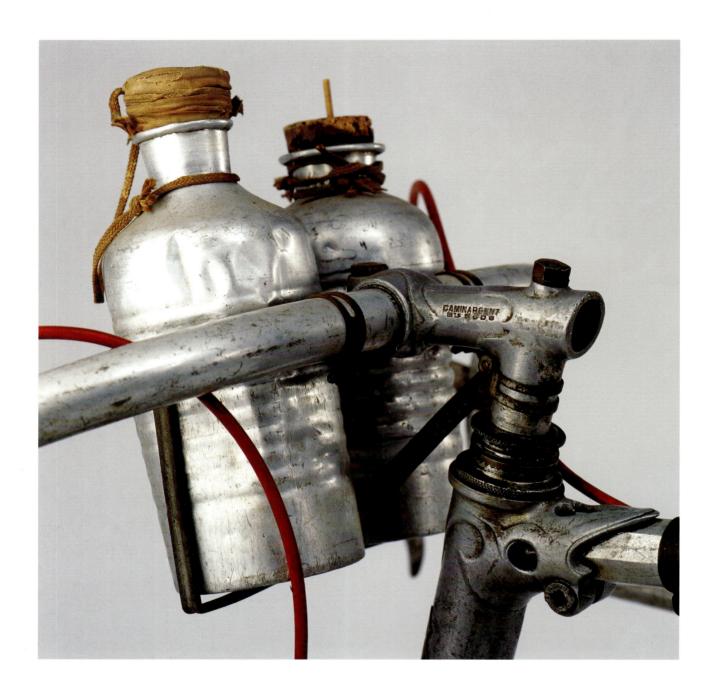

Caminade named his racing model after the great Bordeaux–Paris race, yet there appears to be no record of Caminargents actually being used in serious racing. The frames were said to be very whippy. The Caminargent appears to have been more appealing on paper than on the road.

▲ Allen screws did not yet exist in the 1930s, so Caminade designed his own with a square fitting. Using a single wrench, the bike can be disassembled into its individual lugs and tubes.

In 1933, Stronglight introduced the first modern aluminum cranks ▶ with a square taper, the precursor of most modern cranks. The tapers of the original cranks on this bike are worn, so the cranks sit further inward on the bottom bracket spindle than they did when new.

Tandem Hour Record
Maurice Richard

The ultimate cycling competition is the hour record. A single rider circles the track at maximum effort for a full hour. The conditions are the same for all riders, so there is little doubt about who is strongest. Every top athlete at least considers attacking the hour record, but not all succeed, and some relatively unknown riders do well in this test that does not require climbing skills or tactics.

In 1933, Maurice Richard covered 44.777 km in one hour to claim the hour record for France for the first time in 20 years. Two years later, Guiseppe Olmo improved upon that performance, but in 1936, Richard traveled to the famous Vigorelli velodrome in Milan, where he became the first to push the record beyond 45 km. Earlier that year, Richard and his partner Dayen had set a new hour record on the tandem. With two riders powering a machine of roughly the same wind resistance as a single bike, they naturally went faster than Richard alone, and covered 48.668 km in the hour.

These record runs were sponsored by Cycles Delangle, a large Parisian firm specializing in high-end bicycles. Their program included a variety of machines, from delivery bikes to professional racing bikes. Many of their bikes featured well-made frames with top-of-the-line specifications. Delangle's catalogue proudly proclaimed that 56 world records had been set on their machines.

The seal on the seat lug of Maurice Richard's hour record tandem ▸ was attached by custom's officials to prove upon return from foreign trips that this was the same bike that had left France earlier.

The tandem shown here is the actual machine that Richard and Dayen rode during their hour record. At first glance, it seems to differ in minor details to the one shown in the catalogue photo of the hour record (painted head tube, extended rear seat lug), but the decal placement is exactly the same, down to the slightly crooked "Delangle" decal on the front down tube. It appears that the catalogue image was retouched, and some of the details were lost in the process. Built from standard-diameter Reynolds H.M. tubing, the tandem weighs 16.5 kg (36.3 lbs.).

The single bike shown on the next pages is newer than the tandem. Its lug shape and specification corresponds to Delangle's 1939/1940 catalogue. The frame is made from Reynolds "531 H.M." tubing, and equipped with lightweight components. As a result of all this technology, the bike weighs just 8.1 kg (17.8 lbs.). It is in delightfully original condition, down to the superlight handmade track tires. With new tires and the right rider aboard, perhaps it could still set an hour record today, almost 70 years after it was built.

Trois grands vaincus du Tour de France 1948 dans l'ascension du col de Porte : (de gauche à droite) René Vietto, Apo Lazaridès, qui pousse Vietto en difficulté, et Jean Robic, le vainqueur de 1947...

LES GRANDS VAINCUS DU TOUR 48

A Superlight Bike for a Tour de France Climber
René Vietto

René Vietto burst into the limelight during the 1934 Tour de France. Only 20 years old, he surprised everybody when he dropped his competitors on the hardest climbs. As a junior member of the team, he was a domestique and had to sacrifice first his front wheel and, the next day, his entire bike, for his team leader Antonin Magne, who had mechanical problems. Magne won the Tour, but Vietto might have won if he had been able to ride his own race. France was fascinated by a photo of the dejected René Vietto sitting on a stone wall, with no support van in sight, as his hopes to win the Tour ran through his fingers.

After this promising debut, Vietto progressed steadily, and finally wore the Yellow Jersey during the 1939 Tour de France. He kept it for 16 stages, but in the end, had to settle for second behind Sylvère Maes. World War II interrupted racing, and the next Tour de France was held in 1947. Vietto again was one of the favorites, and he wore the Yellow Jersey for 15 stages. But in the end, he finished fifth.

René Vietto now was 34, and time was running out. For the 1948 Tour de France, he had two superlight bikes built by Nicola Barra, one for himself (shown here) and one for his domestique Apo Lazaridès. Barra had introduced his welded aluminum frames in 1936. They had proven their worth in many cyclotouring competitions, and their light weight was seductive for a small climber like Vietto. Vietto also used Stronglight aluminum cranks, and aluminum brakes. Even with a steel seatpost and Simplex derailleurs, the bike weighs just 8.0 kg (17.6 lb.).

◀ René Vietto (left) on his superlight Barra during the 1948 Tour de France, pushed by his friend Apo Lazaridès. Jean Robic, winner in 1947, also is suffering. The typical Barra fork crown is clearly visible on Vietto's bike. (Courtesy R. Henry)

Alas, the superlight bike did not help Vietto, who could do no better than finish 17th, 1:43 hours behind winner Gino Bartali. Blaming the bike would not be fair: Apo Lazaridès rode his Barra to a second place at that year's world championships.

After the Tour, Vietto returned the bike to Barra's shop. Like most racers, he kept his custom handlebars and stem (and probably his saddle), which he transferred from one bike to the next. Another customer, a Monsieur Duval, saw the bike and asked what would happen to it. When he learned that it was for sale, he bought it on the spot.

▲ The aluminum tubes are ovalized at the bottom bracket to increase the stiffness of the frame.

Italians in the Tour de France
Fiorenzo Magni, Gino Bartali, Fausto Coppi

In the spring of 1949, Alfredo Binda was not a happy man. The retired champion was the manager of the Italian national "A" team for the Tour de France. His problem was not a lack of talent, but too much of it: Italy was home to two of the world's best cyclists, Gino Bartali and Fausto Coppi. To Binda's chagrin, Coppi and Bartali were bitter rivals. At the 1948 World Championships, they had marked each other, unwilling to work together. Focused only on each other, they were left behind by the peloton and abandoned the race in disgrace.

Italy was split in their support for one or the other. Bartali, "the pious one," appealed to traditional Italy. He was deeply religious and lived a simple life. On the bike, he suffered. Coppi was more mundane. On the bike, he looked like he was barely touching the pedals. His supporters were progressives, who wanted to bring Italy into the modern age. Thus, the rivalry between the two "campionissimi" reflected the split of the larger Italian society.

◂ The bike shown on these pages was one of Fiorenzo Magni's 1948 Wilier Triestina bikes. It was similar to the bike he used in 1949 (historic photo above), except that Magni used a Simplex front derailleur in 1949. (Historic photo courtesy Aldo Ross.)

▲ Shifting the Campagnolo Cambio Corsa requires opening the rear quick release. Teeth in dropouts and hub axle mesh to ensure that the wheel remains centered in the frame as it rolls backward or forward to adjust the chain tension.

All this weighed on Alfredo Binda as he prepared for the Tour de France. Coppi had won the 1949 Giro d'Italia, and Bartali had won the previous year's Tour de France. Each believed that they should be the team leader, and their claims were equally valid. Binda spent all spring pleading with the two "campionissimi" to work together for the greater good of the Italian national team. When Binda thought that things were under control, Bartali told the press that he had no intention of working with Coppi.

Binda had to start all over again. To make matters worse, Coppi insisted on racing with modern Simplex derailleurs, whereas Binda preferred the traditional Cervino. The rules of the Tour de France stipulated that each team used just one type of derailleur, but Binda was able to get an exemption from the organizers.

Finally, an uneasy truce was negotiated, and the team took the train to Paris. Coppi and his domestiques sat at one end of the train, and Bartali and his men at the other. Presumably in the middle was Fiorenzo Magni, who led Italy's "B" team.

As the Tour entered the mountains, it was Magni who stole the limelight, when he took the yellow jersey on stage 10 and kept it for six stages. In the mean time, Coppi had crashed and broken his bike. The team car with Coppi's spare bike was near Bartali, and it took a while until Coppi could get under way again. Demoralized, Coppi finished the stage eighteen minutes behind the leaders. He talked of abandoning the race, but his "gregari" from the Bianchi team convinced him to continue.

On the classic alpine stage from Cannes to Briançon, Coppi and Bartali rode away from the field at the foot of the Izoard. The two leaders of the Italian team climbed so swiftly that they gained four minutes in just 20 kilometers. Coppi punctured on the climb, but Bartali waited for him. On the descent, it was Bartali's turn to have a flat tire, and Coppi waited. On the last climb to the imposing citadel of Briançon, Bartali drew ahead and won the stage. It was his 35th birthday, and he put on the yellow jersey. Coppi moved up to second place, and Fiorenzo Magni was more than 12 minutes behind.

The next day, the spectacle repeated itself. Coppi and Bartali broke away, and the field could not match their pace. Then Bartali fell and twisted his ankle. Coppi anxiously waited for his teammate, until Binda told him to ride ahead. Coppi flew through the remaining 42 km of the stage in his inimitable style. Now it was Coppi's turn in the yellow jersey. He kept it until the finish. Bartali finished second. All of Italy was overjoyed by this success, not least team manager Alfredo Binda.

◂ Gino Bartali's bike from the 1949 Tour de France.

▾ Bartali's bike was equipped with many components labeled for his brand, but made by other manufacturers.

▲ Fausto Coppi (front) and Gino Bartali were rivals when the 1949 Tour de France started, but they worked together to place first and second in the race. (Photo: Miroir Archives Photosport International)

One lever controls the spring tension of the chain tensioner under the ▶ bottom bracket, the other operates the shifter fork on the chainstay.

▲ Unlike the earlier Vittoria Margherita with its shifter paddles above the chainstay (see p. 54), the Cervino on Bartali's 1949 bike no longer required backpedaling to shift. In 1949, Campagnolo's quick release had become generally accepted in the professional peloton.

drivetrain's friction. The Cervino allowed him to keep the chain running loosely, almost as freely as with the Campagnolo Cambio Corsa, yet he was able to pedal forward while shifting.

Fausto Coppi's Bianchi matches his impeccably tailored suits and modern outlook. The lugs are thinned, profiled and filed to perfection. The geometry has a steeper head angle and less trail than Bartali's traditional machine. The Simplex derailleur shifts with just a flick of the lever and a slight letting up on the pedals.

Despite their differences, all three bikes performed exceptionally under their riders, enabling each to wear the Yellow Jersey during the 1949 Tour de France.

◂ Many Bianchis were equipped with an integrated headset.

◂ Fausto Coppi's Bianchi from the 1949 Tour de France.

The bikes of the three Italian leaders of the 1949 Tour de France showcase their riders' different approaches to racing. Magni's bike shown here is not his Tour de France machine, but a similar bike he used for other races in 1948. The frame appears well-made from quality tubing, but little time was spent on filing the lugs. To shift Campagnolo's Cambio Corsa derailleur, Magni opened the quick release with the long lever, then backpedaled and moved the chain with the short lever and its attached shifter fork. The rear wheel's toothed axle rolled backward or forward in the toothed dropouts to take up the chain slack. Shifting required some skill, and Magni had to backpedal while changing gears. However, the derailleur did not touch the chain except when shifting, so there was no added friction, and nothing to go wrong even if the rider crashed. In fact, Magni was well aware of the limitations of this setup. During some stages, presumably those that required a lot of shifting, he used a Simplex rear derailleur like Coppi.

Gino Bartali's bike has an old-fashioned geometry with a relatively shallow head angle and generous trail. The Cervino derailleur is a relative of the 1930s Super Champion (see p. 54). To shift, Bartali first released the chain tension with one shift lever, then he operated the second shift lever to move the chain with the shifter fork under the chainstay. Finally, he re-tensioned the chain. Like many racers, Bartali apparently was convinced that a spring-loaded chain tensioner greatly increased the

▲ Fausto Coppi crests the Izoard during the decisive stage from Cannes to Briançon.
(Photo: Miroir Archives – Photosport International)

Newspaper Courier Racing

Until the 1960s, newspapers in Paris were transported from the printing presses to the newsstands by bicycle couriers. These "porteurs de presse" were paid per trip. With numerous editions of each paper per day, the best "runs" earned their owners a very substantial income. Many of these porteurs were amateur and semi-professional racers, who loved cycling and competition. Their work allowed them to train by riding their bicycles most of the day, while earning more money than most professional racers.

Perhaps it was obvious to organize a championship of the newspaper couriers every year. This was a hotly contested race. The main roads of Paris were closed for the race, and the daily newspapers reported the event in detail. The race started in the newspaper district in the center of Paris, then circled the old city on the "outer boulevards," and finished with a climb up the cobbled streets of Montmartre. Union rules forbid newspaper carriers from using multiple speeds, and each competitor had to carry 15 kg (33 lbs.) of newspapers. At roughly the half-way point, the load had to be exchanged for fresh newspapers. Despite these obstacles, the fastest racers covered the 38 km (24 miles) in just under an hour, including the stop to exchange the newspapers.

While the porteurs' workbikes used wide tires and large fenders to keep the riders and loads dry in Paris' frequent drizzle, serious porteurs competed on racing bikes equipped with large custom-built front racks and fenders to make them look like real "porteur" bicycles. Tubular tires were not permitted, so riders used hand-made clinchers to gain a competitive edge.

The original porteur racing bikes are long gone. After the racing finished in the 1960s, the front racks were removed, and the bikes became regular racing bikes. The bicycle shown was recreated from a 1951 René Herse fixed-gear training bicycle and an original rack made by Herse for one of Robert Prestat's racing bikes.

▲ The "Criterium des Porteurs de Presse" 1948 soon after the start.
(Photo: Joel Metz Collection)

▲ Robert Prestat was one of the most senior "porteurs" with one of the best runs. This enabled him to afford the latest custom bicycles from René Herse, the best constructeur in Paris. Here Prestat arrives at the Porte d'Orléans to exchange newspapers during the 1950 race. Lyli Herse, daughter of the constructeur, and Louderc assist in the exchange. Prestat finished third, narrowly beaten in the sprint for second place.
(Photos: Jac, courtesy Lyli Herse)

Three Custom Bikes for an Independent Racer
Georges Baudin

Georges Baudin was an independent racer. He had no sponsor to pay his salary, but instead relied on starting and prize money to earn his living. He competed on the road and on the track. Baudin carefully selected the tools of his trade. He owned three different bikes, and for each, he had an identical back-up bike, making a total of six bikes.

Baudin's road and track frames were made by Bianco, a legendary "cadreur" (framebuilder) in Paris, who supplied many professionals with frames. Like many cadreurs, Bianco only sold bare frames, which usually were painted in the colors of the riders' sponsors. Georges Baudin simply had his painted blue.

▲ Georges Baudin at speed on his Bastide stayer bike.
(Photo: Jean-C. Picochi, courtesy H. March)

For motorpaced stayer events, Baudin had a pair of 1930s Bastide stayer machines. In post-war France, no maker offered new stayer machines, so old Bastides were highly prized and continued to be raced.

The frame of Baudin's road bike is similar in concept to Coppi's bike from the 1949 Tour de France (p. 88), but in just a few years, key components have changed. When Tullio Campagnolo designed his Gran Sport parallelogram derailleurs, he no longer worried about straight chain runs and low chain tension, but his derailleurs were more reliable and durable than all other systems. Mafac's Racer brakes set the standard for stopping power and modulation. Stronglight's aluminum cranks had been introduced in 1932, but it took almost 20 years until they found widespread acceptance among top racers. These innovations defined racing bikes for decades to come.

Baudin did not follow modern trends in every respect. He preferred steel for his handlebars, stem and seatpost. And Baudin's track bike still uses cottered steel cranks, because weight matters relatively little on the track. Like many racers, Baudin preferred the narrower tread (horizontal distance between the cranks) of the old-fashioned steel cranks, as they facilitated his spin on the banked ovals.

Baudin's Bastide stayer bike was repainted to match his other machines. It is a 1930s model, newer than the stayer shown on p. 41, and without the reinforcement at the lower headtube joint. Georges Baudin took his racing seriously, and his bicycles reflected this. Each was the very best available in its category at the time.

▲ The Campagnolo hubs (made by FB) were laced to Mavic aluminum rims with superlight 2.0/1.6 mm butted spokes.

▲ The Bianco track bike used cottered steel cranks, which allowed a narrower stance (tread) of the pedals.

▲ The Bastide stayer bike dates from the 1930s, but still was state-of-the-art in the 1950s.

Georges Baudin at the start of a stayer race. ▶
(Photo: A. Roques, courtesy Helen March)

BASTIDE STAYER

A Production Bike for an Amateur Racer

For many amateurs, who only dabbled in racing, a custom bicycle was unaffordable. For these riders, most French manufacturers offered very competent production machines at significantly lower prices. This Rochet Super Special was raced by such an amateur, who probably had little hope of earning prize money.

The frame is made from quality tubing. Chrome-plating on lugs and fork adds a touch of class, but there is no mistaking it for a finely crafted frame from a top "cadreur" (framebuilder). The components were a tier below the most expensive equipment. Even so, there was nothing on this bike that would hold back a racer, and many professionals rode on similar equipment, as they were bound by sponsors' contracts. The Simplex JUY 51 rear derailleur incorporates an automatic adjuster for the chain tension, operated via a second cable that unwinds the tension spring when shifting to a larger cog. The lever-operated front derailleur shifted quickly and reliably over the closely spaced chainrings. The LAM brakes did not stop as well as the new Mafacs, but racing is about speed, and not about stopping. The Exceltoo aluminum hubs were laced to quality Record rims to make durable wheels. With the money saved on the bike, the rider could buy a set of hand-made tubular tires, which improved the bike's performance more significantly than high-end components.

▲ The Simplex JUY 51 derailleur keeps the chain tension constant. One cable moves the derailleur cage via the small chain, while a second cable unwinds the tension spring as the derailleur shifts to a bigger cog. (The front chainrings are so close in size that the chain tension is unaffected by front shifts.) Both shifter cables are joined above the chainstay, so the rider has to operate only a single lever.

Paris-Brest-Paris
Lucien Détée, Gilbert Bulté

In 1950s France, bicycle racing was mostly a working-class sport. For many racers, prize money and professional contracts provided an alternative to the toil in factories and coal mines.

Middle-class riders, who enjoyed the sport of cycling without aspirations of earning a living on two wheels, rarely became racers. Instead, they joined the cyclotourists. As amateurs in the true sense of the word, most of these cyclists had well-paying careers and rode their bikes strictly for enjoyment.

If anything, this made the cyclotourists more enthusiastic about their equipment, and many had the means to buy their dream bicycles. The best bicycles in the 1940s and 1950s were not racing machines, but cyclotouring bikes. The rules of cyclotouring competition mandated fenders, rack and lights. So-called "constructeurs" built fully integrated bikes, not just frames. Virtually all components of the bike were conceived as part of the whole machine, rather than as a collection of bolt-on accessories. When the constructeurs were dissatisfied with commercially available bottom brackets, stems, derailleurs, brakes or racks, they made their own parts. Many innovations developed by these constructeurs found their way onto racing bikes after they had proven themselves on cyclotouring bikes. These include aluminum frames, oversize tubing, vertical dropouts, braze-ons for shift levers and derailleurs, cantilever brakes, aluminum cranks, parallelogram derailleurs and cartridge bearings. With all this innovation and a completely integrated design, the best French cyclotouring bikes were very elegant and often lighter than racing bikes, but also more expensive.

René Herse was considered the best of the constructeurs. After an early career in aircraft construction, he introduced innovative bicycle components in the late 1930s. A few years later, he began offering complete bicycles. Herse and his wife were avid tandemists, and the machines built for two were his specialty.

Like most cyclists, cyclotourists were not averse to a little competition. Randonneuring provided a way to challenge oneself against the clock, but also against other riders. René Herse supported a team of strong riders. These young men and women competed in events like the Poly de Chanteloup hillclimb, the Boucles de la Seine tandem race, and perhaps the most famous of all, the Paris-Brest-Paris randonneur ride.

First held in 1891, Paris-Brest-Paris had started as a professional long-distance race, from France's capital to its westernmost town and back. Unlike in later stage races, the clock did not stop ticking until the riders had covered the entire distance of 1200 km (765 miles). From 1931 onward, randonneurs also tested themselve against this enormous distance. In 1956, the team of Lucien Détée and Gilbert Bulté, both riding for René Herse, decided to try their luck over the long and hilly course.

As the riders lined up at the Porte de Saint-Cloud on the western edge of Paris in the evening of September 5, it started to rain, and a strong wind blew in the riders' faces. From the start, two tandems took the lead: Jo Routens/Jouffrey and Détée/Bulté. The former had placed first in both previous editions of the randonneur PBP and held the current course record. The team of Détée and Bulté had won numerous tandem events in recent years. Both teams were clear favorites in this event.

As the ride began, the two tandems quickly built their lead over the single riders. However, even the tandems took more than 24 hours to reach Brest in the difficult conditions. The veteran Routens knew that there was no hope of breaking his 1951 record of just under 48 hours. On the return trip, Détée and Bulté stopped to eat a hot meal at a checkpoint, which they had pre-ordered on the way out. Routens and Jouffrey continued alone into the second night, but they did not keep their lead for long. Soon the two tandems were back together, and they stayed together all the way back to Paris. Their time, 50:29 hours, was remarkable considering the constant rain and wind. The first single-bike rider, Roger Baumann, also riding for René Herse, took a little over two hours longer.

The winning Herse tandem was Lucien Détée's personal machine. It was built in 1948 as a chrome-plated touring tandem with large front and rear racks for Jacques Bion, a well-known randonneur. With oversized tubing and special hand-made lugs, it provided plenty of stiffness and strength even for a strong team. The tandem-specific geometry made the large machine as nimble as a good racing bike, while the wide tires absorbed road irregularities without the need for suspension. Like most of Herse's top-of-the-line machines, the tandem was equipped with his own cranks, bottom brackets, cantilever brakes, stems, front derailleur and special eccentric shift lever to take up the cable slack of the Cyclo rear derailleur.

▲ The JOS taillight incorporates a reflector in the center. The outer red ring is illuminated by the bulb. The wires to the generator run invisibly inside the frame.

◀ Lucien Détée (left) and Gilbert Bulté at the finish at the Porte de Saint-Cloud in Paris. The photo was taken the morning after the ride, allowing the riders to put on clean clothes and wash up after 50 hours of riding in the rain.
(Photo: Berton; courtesy L. Détée)

Just before Lucien Détée bought the tandem, Herse converted it to a randonneur machine with only a small front rack. It was painted in Herse's trademark blue color. For the long nights of PBP, Herse mounted a large flashlight and a battery-powered taillight, which provided illumination without the drag of the generator. A large handlebar bag held extra clothes and food.

Today, randonneuring officially no longer endorses "competition," but there always will be those who want to see how fast they can complete the course, and who can do it fastest. After all, even cyclotourists are cyclists, and cyclists like a little competition.

▲ To eliminate the resistance of the generator, the tandem was equipped with battery-powered lights. The generator-powered lights served as backups when the batteries were exhausted.

The tandem originally was built as a touring tandem. The front rack ▶ attached to the sides of the fork crown. The lower headset race is oversized to accommodate the tapered steerer tube, which reinforces this highly stressed area. All tubes of the Herse tandem are oversized.

A Cinelli for America
Bruce Waddell

Already on a decline during the 1930s, bicycle racing in North America continued to plummet after World War II, when bicycles were seen as mere children's toys. The sport's popularity began to increase again in the 1960s, now on the road rather than the track. Inspired by the great European races, American racers began to venture into the mountains.

Bruce Waddell was studying engineering at the University of Washington when a fellow student introduced him to cycling and racing. Bruce showed promise, and in 1965, he finished third in the Washington State Road Racing Championships, over a 125-mile (200 km) course in the Cascade Mountains that included three mountain passes. Immediately after the race, Bruce ordered a new bike from the renowned Cupertino Bicycle Shop in California.

Unlike European amateurs, the favorable exchange rate for the U.S. dollar allowed even a student like Waddell to buy the most expensive equipment. His Cinelli Supercorsa was considered the very best bicycle available at the time, and he equipped it with every option recommended by Spence Wolf, the owner of the Cupertino Bicycle Shop.

The classic Campagnolo Record drivetrain was state of the art, with cotterless aluminum cranks and the famous parallelogram derailleurs. Spence Wolf preferred Mafac centerpull brakes for their superior stopping power and Weinmann brake levers, because they featured an integrated quick release. Simply pressing the red button opened the brake wider to facilitate wheel changes.

▲ Bruce Waddell after the 1965 Washington State Championships. (Photo: Dick Taylor)

Spence Wolf was famous for his hand-built wheels, which stayed true much longer than most. The high-flange Campagnolo hubs were laced to superlight Scheeren tubular rims weighing just 275 g. These rims were equipped with small wooden blocks at every spoke hole to prevent the spoke tension from collapsing the thin aluminum walls of the rims. The thin double-butted spokes were tied and soldered to improve the durability of the wheels. While the rear wheel was rebuilt after an accident, the original front wheel still remains perfectly true more than 40 years after it was built.

The Cinelli shows how the classic racing bike was reaching its final form. The frame geometry was similar to that of many 1970s racing bikes. The Campagnolo Record "gruppo" remained the standard for the next two decades. Later incarnations as "Nuovo Record" and "Super Record" used aluminum and titanium to reduce the weight, but on the road, this 1965 Cinelli rides very much like a racing bike from the 1970s. Unfortunately, it never carried Bruce Waddell to the victories he had in mind when he bought the bike. His studies began to take too much time to train seriously, and the Cinelli did not see many miles.

Bruce Waddell taped the gear ratios to his stem. ▶
The front chainrings are only 4 teeth apart, providing half as big a step as the cogs of the freewheel. Rear shifts provide relatively large steps between gears. A front shift allows fine-tuning the gear ratio via a "half-step."

The Cinelli is equipped with the complete 1965 Record "gruppo" ▶ of top-of-the-line components.

The Record derailleur handles the 14-28 freewheel with ease. ▶ It is made from brass and steel, and uses steel pulleys with ball bearings, so it is rather heavy.

Women's World Champion
Geneviève Gambillon

Male racers tend to get most of the headlines, even though women have been racing bicycles since the earliest days of cycling competition. Some female racers won fame by beating not just other women, but also the best of the men in various events. For example, Beryl Burton once held the 12-hour time trial record in Britain, while in France, mixed tandems with Lyli Herse as the stoker often beat the fastest male teams.

After winning 8 French championship titles in the 1950s and 1960s, Lyli Herse retired from racing to coach a women's team, sponsored by her father, the famous constructeur René Herse. This small, close-knit team consisted of a handful of amateur women, who trained from four until six o'clock in the morning before starting their day of work or study. The hard work paid off: Genevieve Gambillon won numerous French championships on road and track, and other team members were not far behind.

The 1972 World Championships were held in Gap in the French Alps. The favorites included the British mother-and-daughter duo of Beryl and Denise Burton, former world champion Audrey McElmury from the United States, as well as the Soviet team with the reigning World Champion Anna Konkina. During the race, six riders broke away on the first lap. The break included all the favorites, as well as the French riders Geneviève Gambillon and Annick Chapron.

As a time trial specialist, Beryl Burton kept the pace high and ensured that the break was not caught by the pack. During each of the last two laps, riders attacked on the climbs without being able to break away. Approaching the finish line, Gambillon was led out by her teammate Annick Chapron. Gambillon timed her sprint perfectly and powered away from the group, crossing the line several bike-lengths ahead of the others.

Two years later, Geneviève Gambillon again displayed her strength by winning the World Championships in Montreal, Canada, where she crossed the finish line first in front of tens of thousands of spectators. Gambillon rode this 1970 René Herse racing bike to both of her World Championship victories, as well as four French championships and numerous other race wins. The bike is very well-built, but the finish work is slightly less refined than that of the best René Herse cyclotouring bikes. It is equipped with French and Swiss components: Huret derailleurs, Weinmann brakes, Maillard hubs and a Stronglight bottom bracket. Cranks and stem were made by René Herse. Genevieve Gambillon remembers this bike as her best-performing bike, which is why she used it for most important races throughout her racing career.

▲ At the 1972 World Championships in Gap, France, G. Gambillon's powerful sprint left little chance to her rivals. At the back of the breakaway, teammate A. Chapron already celebrates after leading out Gambillon. (Photo courtesy L. Herse.)

The Cannibal's Bike for the Triple Crown
Eddy Merckx

By 1974, Eddy Merckx had been the undisputed leader of the professional peloton for six years. During this time, he had won four Tours de France, four Giri d'Italia, two world championships, as well as dozens of one-day classics. He also had set an hour record. Merckx' indomitable will to win had earned him the nickname "The Cannibal," and many racers secretly hoped that Merckx' reign would end, so others could win again.

Even though Merckx was only 29 years old, he may have felt that his best days were behind him. Illness during the spring did not allow him to try and win every race on the 1974 calendar. Instead, he had to focus on the most important events. The "Triple Crown" of bicycle racing refers to the Giro d'Italia, the Tour de France and the World Championships. Nobody ever had won all three events during the same season.

During the spring, Merckx won the Giro d'Italia, then placed first in the Tour of Switzerland, which he used as preparation for the Tour de France. The Tour de France showed Merckx' vulnerability. Six riders beat Merckx in a time trial, but he fought back and won two of the hardest stages in the Alps. This performance secured his fifth win in the Tour de France and equaled the record for the most Tour wins, held by Jacques Anquetil.

▲ Merckx leads the charge up the hill of Mont Royal on his way to winning the 1974 world championships.
(Photo: Ken Johnson)

To win the Triple Crown, Merckx now needed to win the world championships, held that year in Montréal, Canada. Merckx pulled off that feat as well, and thus defended his claim to being the best bicycle racer the world had ever seen.

The bike shown here was Merckx' bike for the 1974 World Championships. It was built by Ugo De Rosa, even though it is labeled Eddy Merckx. At the time, Merckx licensed his name to several bicycle makers, like Falcon in England and Kessels in Belgium. Merckx' machine had little in common with these mass-produced bicycles. Ugo de Rosa was a master of his craft, and the bike was carefully built to Merckx' exact specifications. Merckx was very concerned about the fit of his bike. He once famously stopped during a race to adjust his bike. The classic frame is complemented with Campagnolo Nuovo Record components, which had become the standard racing equipment of the 1970s. Always concerned about light weight, Merckx had grooves machined into the large chainring and stem. Nevertheless, with a stiff frame to withstand the immense power of the Cannibal, the bike was no lightweight, tipping the scales at 11.0 kg (24.3 lbs.).

In 1975, Merckx gave this bicycle to the Pope, who eventually passed it on to "The Flying Priest," Battista Mondiu. After riding it for a few years, the priest donated the bike to the Chapel of the Madonna del Ghisallo, which is dedicated to bicycle racing.

▲ Eddy Merckx' frame was built by Ugo De Rosa, whose frames usually featured a heart cut into the bottom bracket shell.

Time Trialing in Style
J.P Weigle

With the resurgence of bicycle racing in North America during the 1960s, American cyclists became intrigued by the almost mythical craft of framebuilding. Only few American builders still were practicing this craft, so young riders looked to Europe when they decided to learn how to build frames.

One of these riders was 23-year-old Peter Weigle. In 1973, he worked at Witcomb in Britain for seven months to learn about building bicycles. During his stay, Weigle became an avid time trialist. Time trials had a strong tradition in Britain, whereas massed-start road races were relatively rare. Weigle was greatly impressed by the purpose-built time trial bikes of the best riders. At the time, there was a widespread belief that even over a flat time trial course, weight was the most important impediment to speed, so time trial machines were built with the lightest components available. Many riders removed additional weight by drilling and machining their components. The special frames with their modified and polished components were a sight to behold. These competition-bred machines gave their riders confidence and intimidated the competition. Weigle likened them to "war paint."

As an unpaid intern, Weigle could only dream about racing one of these gleaming machines. He competed on a standard ten-speed road bike with heavy wheels. This did not prevent him from placing well in the British time trials, which were run as handicap events. The handicaps were assigned based on previous performances. Weigle kept improving more than the handicappers anticipated, so he often "beat the handicap" and won prize money at these events.

▲ The bike holder lets go, and Weigle is off for the 1975 Connecticut State Time Trial Championship. He won the 25-mile event. (Photo courtesy of Peter Weigle)

In 1973, Weigle returned to the United States and worked at Witcomb USA. He built this time trial bike for himself in 1975, emulating the machines he had admired when he raced in Britain. Every part was carefully selected, and many components were modified by drilling, machining, re-shaping and polishing. To eliminate the weight of lugs, Weigle fillet-brazed the frame from Reynolds 531 Competition tubing. The lightest Weinmann brakes were combined with drilled Mafac levers. Campagnolo high-flange hubs were laced with just 24 spokes to superlight Scheeren Weltmeister rims. Even the unpadded saddle was drilled to save a few grams. With its gleaming paint and contrasting accents on the components, this bike was "war paint" indeed.

The bike was not just for show. Peter Weigle rode it to victory in the 1975 Connecticut State Time Trial Championship. When Witcomb USA closed its doors in 1977, Weigle began building bikes under his own name. He repainted his time trial bike and labeled it with his decals. So it finally became what it always had been: a very special J. P. Weigle bicycle.

An American in Europe
Greg LeMond

Starting in the 1970s, a number of American racers went to Europe to race as amateurs. A few of them soon turned professional. In 1981, Jonathan Boyer became the first American to race in the Tour de France. Riding for the French Renault-Gitane team, he supported Bernard Hinault, who won his third Tour de France that year (see photo p. 5). Renault-Gitane's team director, Cyrille Guimard, saw the potential of American racers. He had noticed an American amateur racer, who had displayed the spirit and courage that Guimard liked in his young racers. Together with Tour champion Bernard Hinault, he traveled to Carson City, Nevada, to woo Greg LeMond to the Renault-Gitane team.

LeMond's first year in Europe was not without challenges. Just 19 years old, he struggled with a new language, unfamiliar food and homesickness. He also had to get used to racing in Europe, where speeds were high and competition was cut-throat. But young Greg quickly found his feet, and his incredible career took off.

This team-issue Gitane was the first bike of LeMond's professional career. The frame was finely crafted in Gitane's racing shop. It is equipped with standard Campagnolo Super Record components, which were the latest incarnation of the classic 1960s Record components. Knowing that wheels matter more than anything else on a racing bike, Gitane's mechanics carefully glued handmade tubular tires onto expensive Mavic SSC Paris-Roubaix rims. Far from being fancy, this bike was a tool. It served Greg LeMond well as he launched his professional career. Just a few months after signing with Renault-Gitane, he won a stage in the 1981 Tour de L'Oise. In July, while Boyer and Hinault were racing in the Tour de France, LeMond returned to the U.S., to race in the Nevada City Classic. After winning this prestigious race for the third time in a row, he left the Gitane bicycle with his parents when he returned to Europe.

In his first year as a European professional, Greg LeMond returned ▶ to his home state and won the Nevada City Classic for the third time in a row. (Photo: Ted Mock)

LeMond's meteoric rise took him to the highest peaks of professional cycling. Only two years later, he used a similar Gitane to become World Champion. He then went on to win three Tours de France and one more world championship title. Thanks to LeMond's successes, American racers gained respect in the professional peloton, and bicycle racing became an accepted and even popular sport in the United States.

Racing Across America
John Marino

While Greg LeMond was living the hard life of a young professional racer in Europe, bicycle racing in the United States became increasingly popular. Unlike Europe's emphasis on road races, criteriums (races around a short circuit) were the mainstay of American racing.

A few renegades had different ideas. John Marino organized the longest bicycle race the world had seen: 2968 miles (4777 km) non-stop from Santa Monica on the Pacific coast of the United States to New York on the Atlantic coast. The Great American Bike Race (GABR), as it was called, was a novel concept. Unlike the French randonneur events (p. 111), which encouraged riders to be un-supported and self-sufficient, GABR racers each were followed by a car that provided support.

The inaugural race saw four starters, including the organizer, John Marino. All four finished, with Lon Haldeman winning the event in 9 days and 20 hours. Marino was a distant fourth, crossing the finish line in New York almost three days later, where he received a hero's welcome from his fellow competitors and the media.

▲ At the start for the first race across America in Santa Monica, California (left to right): Lon Haldeman, John Howard, Michael Shermer, John Marino. (Photo courtesy Chris Kostman)

The Great America Bike Race was renamed Race Across America (RAAM) the following year. It has captivated long-distance cyclists ever since.

Marino's ride was sponsored by Huffy, then the largest mass producer of inexpensive bicycles in the United States. Many of Huffy's team bikes, including those ridden by the U.S. team at the 1984 Olympics, were built by Mike Melton, a framebuilder from South Carolina.

Marino's bike is a radical departure from traditional European racing bikes, which had not changed much in more than 20 years. As one would expect from the country that put the first man on the moon, the Huffy is very high-tech. Realizing the importance of aerodynamics for a single cyclist, Melton used airfoil-shaped frame tubes to streamline the bike.

The shift levers are placed on top of the down tube, where they are sheltered behind the headtube. All cables run inside the frame. The wheels are equipped with airfoil-shaped rims. Even the seatpost is profiled to "cheat the wind." To improve the rider's pedaling efficiency, the Shimano Dura-Ace cranks place the pedal bearings inside the cranks, which allows lowering the pedal so that its pivot is in line with the balls of the rider's feet. The cassette rear hub combines hub and freewheeling mechanism into a single unit. This reduces the risk of breaking rear axles with 6-speed freewheels that require a longer axle overhang.

Suntour had modified the standard racing derailleurs by slanting the parallelogram, so the jockey pulley followed the contour of the freewheel. This dramatically improved shifting. Today, all derailleurs use this design.

While it looked impressive, this "bicycle of the future" turned out to be a bit of a blind alley. Builders and racers soon realized that it was more important to streamline the rider than to worry about minute details of the bicycle.

▲ To improve the wheel's aerodynamics, the Dura-Ace AX cassette hub has countersunk spoke holes. All spokes are inserted from the inside. The spoke holes on the right side are unevenly spaced to allow using the same spoke length as on the left side.

Mountain Bike Pioneers
Jacquie Phelan

Cyclists have been riding over rough terrain since the invention of bicycles. Country roads and mountain passes remained unpaved until well into the 20th century. And in Europe, cyclocross has been an established sport since at least the early 1900s. Even so, most cyclists preferred smooth roads, until mountain biking took the world by storm.

Starting in the 1970s with rebuilt Schwinn balloon-tire bikes, the first mountain bike races went down the famous Repack Road on Mount Tamalpais in Marin County. Repack's name alludes to a post-race ritual of replenishing the vaporized grease in the coaster brakes. When these pioneers tired of pushing or trucking their bikes uphill, they added derailleurs to their "clunkers." This allowed them to tackle all kinds of terrain, and the "mountain bike" was born.

▲ Jacquie Phelan at a race in China Camp State Park, Marin County, in 1985. (Photo: Gordon Bainbridge)

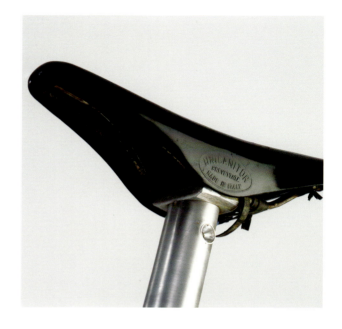

Many of the early mountain bikers did not take their sport too seriously, and the first mountain bike races often resembled rolling parties. This did not prevent the best riders from working hard at beating the competition. The queen among the early mountain bike racers was Jacquie Phelan. She competed successfully with men until there finally were enough female mountain bikers to run separate races for women. Jacquie then won the first three NORBA (National Off-Road Bicycle Association) championships in 1983, 1984 and 1985. She remembers those years fondly: "I enjoyed riding off-road from the moment I was ushered up to the top of Mt. Tam on my Peugeot PX-10 road bike in 1978! Everyone was racing in the 1980s because it was fun, and we loved to be out of doors."

Jacquie Phelan's bike "Otto" was built by Charlie Cunningham. Where most pioneering mountain bikes were a mixture of European racing and American balloon-tire technology, Cunningham used his engineering background to craft truly innovative machines. His frames were welded from oversize aluminum tubing and heat-treated. To complement these unique frames, Cunningham fabricated light and stiff forks, oversize seatposts and direct-clamp stems. His roller-cam brakes provided excellent stopping power. He designed and patented grease ports with internal seals for many components to facilitate lubrication and increase longevity without the need for frequent disassembly.

Most early mountain bikes used slack head angles and high geometric trail figures inspired by balloon-tire bikes, even though these geometries had not been intended for spirited riding. Imitating motorcycles, mountain bikers adopted wide, flat handlebars. Contrasting this, Cunningham preferred steeper head angles, less trail and relatively narrow drop handlebars. Riders found his bicycles easier to steer around obstacles on the trail.

Cunningham's bicycles worked very well, but their high cost, limited production and lack of advertising stood in the way of widespread recognition. To bring his innovative components to a larger audience, Cunningham, together with Steve Potts and Mark Slate, founded Wilderness Trail Bikes (WTB) in 1983. He also licensed his Grease-Guard technology to the Japanese component manufacturer Suntour.

Today, Jacquie Phelan and Charlie Cunningham still live at the foot of Mt. Tamalpais. As the founder of the WOMBATS (Women's Mountain Bike & Tea Society), Jacquie encourages women and girls to try off-road cycling.

Bringing Science to the Hour Record

Francesco Moser

When Eddy Merckx set the hour record in 1972, many believed that his record would stand forever. The "Cannibal" had suffered terribly during his ride, and there was nobody who could ride harder than Merckx. However, some believed that advances in science offered an opportunity to improve upon Merckx' performance.

Francesco Moser was one of the dominant riders of the late 1970s and early 1980s. As a tall, powerful rider, he did very well in the tough one-day classics. After becoming world champion early in his career, he won on the fabled cobblestones of Paris-Roubaix three times in a row. In 1983, he realized that he would not be able to win the Giro d'Italia or the Tour de France, because his imposing physique made him less suited to long climbs. The hour record gave his cycling new focus.

To beat the invincible Merckx, Moser's team completely re-thought the bicycle. Merckx' bike had been built by Ernest Colnago, who was concerned mostly with light weight, following the tradition of the time trial machines of the day. Moser's scientific advisers knew that aerodynamics, and not weight, provided the most important resistance the rider had to overcome at 50 km/h (31.3 mph).

▲ Francesco Moser had 15 different bicycles built for his hour record attempt. Here he is riding one of the spare bikes during a track omnium in Leicester, England, a few months after his hour record.

On January 23, 1984, Francesco Moser rode this bicycle to ▶ a new hour record.

Moser's team calculated that their rider would beat Merckx' record by just 67 meters. With a margin this small, even the smallest advantage was important. Moser's bike for the hour record combined numerous innovative features that had been developed for track racing. A smaller front wheel allowed a more radically inclined position of the rider. Disc wheels brought further aerodynamic improvements. The rear wheel was slightly larger than standard, because a larger wheel rolls easier over irregularities in the track surface and thus has a lower rolling resistance.

Wind tunnel tests had shown that for Francesco Moser, a rearward riding position was more aerodynamic and made it easier to control the bike at speed. Aerodynamic fine-tuning included a special chainring that filled the spaces between the crankarm spider. The cranks themselves were reprofiled. Moser's shoes were firmly attached to the pedals, eliminating toeclips and straps. And since it cannot hurt to have a lighter bike, the bottom bracket was equipped with a titanium spindle. A classic touch were the superlight tubular track tires with silk casings, which were very similar to the ones used by Merckx 12 years earlier.

Moser's personal preparation was as scientific as his bicycle. A rigorous training schedule was complemented with blood doping, which at the time was not yet illegal.

After three months of preparation, the team set out to Mexico City, where the thin air at more than 2200 m (7200 ft) elevation provided less resistance. Moser's first attempt at the record exceeded all expectations. Far from eking out a narrow record, Moser bettered Merckx' distance by a large margin and became the first rider to surpass the magic 50 km mark. After the ride, Moser thought he could have gone faster. Four days later, he returned to the velodrome to improve upon his performance. This time, a light wind spoiled the attempt, but Moser persevered. He suffered tremendously. His record of 51.151 km improved upon his first attempt by more than 300 m. Moser had ridden 1720 meters further than Merckx during his one-hour ride. This was the greatest improvement the hour record had seen in its history.

After Moser returned to Italy, he found that his preparation for the hour record had made him stronger than ever before. So strong in fact, that he finally realized his dream of winning the Giro d'Italia that spring.

The Americans Are Coming!
Andy Hampsten

Andy Hampsten went to Europe in 1985 to race as a professional. Almost immediately, the gifted climber won a stage in the Giro d'Italia, which led to a spot on Bernard Hinault's team. In 1986, Hampsten won the Tour of Switzerland and helped Greg LeMond (see p. 136) to become the first American to win the Tour de France. Hampsten rode so well that he placed fourth overall. Americans made their mark on European racing.

Many felt it was time for an American team to race in Europe. Sponsorship was provided by the 7-Eleven convenience store chain, and Hampsten was signed as the team leader. He won the 1987 Tour of Switzerland during the first year of the team's existence. The following year, Hampsten showed his brilliant climbing at the Giro d'Italia. He won a mountain stage and placed second in another. With eight stages to go, he was in fifth place overall. With more mountain stages ahead, Hampsten was a contender for the overall victory.

The story of the decisive stage has become part of cycling's lore. Two feet of snow fell on the Gavia Pass, and most racers were woefully unprepared. 7-Eleven team manager Mike Neel rushed to various ski shops that morning, where he bought winter gloves and hats for his entire team. Helped by the warm clothing, Hampsten finished second on the stage, but gained so much time on the favorites that the overall victory of the Giro d'Italia was his. Hampsten's record shows that his Giro win was no fluke. Even on a warm and dry day, he had the ability to outclimb the race leaders on the 16-percent slopes of the Gavia. As if to make that point, Hampsten won the uphill time trial a few days later as he defended his lead.

Andy Hampsten rode his Landshark most of the 1988 season, here in the Tour de France.
(Photo: John Pierce, Photosport International)

LANDSHARK

lever after each shift. Index shifting hardly provided an advantage to skilled professional racers, but the technology put modern high-performance bicycles within the reach of many casual riders who were intimidated by derailleurs.

After this promising start, Hampsten's career ended perhaps prematurely when EPO doping arrived in the peloton. Suddenly, the winged climber no longer could keep up with second-rate riders on mountain stages. After Hampsten retired, the 7-Eleven team continued under Motorola sponsorship. In 1992, the team signed another promising young American: Lance Armstrong.

◂ Hampsten's bike was one of the first to be equipped with clipless pedals, which had been pioneered by Look and the French La Vie Claire team in 1985.

▾ In 1985, Shimano introduced the first modern indexing system and changed how cyclists shift.

The 7-Eleven team was sponsored by Huffy, but most of the team bikes were built by Serotta. The frame of Andy's Serotta team bike broke in a spring race. Andy then asked John Slawta of Landshark to build him a different frame. Hampsten's bike is similar to the Landsharks that Slawta built for his customers at the time. The frame was made from ultralight Tange Prestige tubing with walls that were just 0.4 mm thick in the center of the tubes. It is equipped with Shimano's Dura-Ace components. After the innovative Dura-Ace AX group (p. 140) had flopped commercially, Shimano presented a classic group as a replacement. Most of the 1985 Dura-Ace components were little more than refined copies of Campagnolo's Super Record, but the drivetrain was revolutionary. The rear derailleur combined Suntour's slant parallelogram with Simplex' spring-loaded upper pivot. Using Computer Aided Design (CAD), the derailleur was fine-tuned to work with a ratcheting shift lever to provide secure, instant shifts without the need to overshift or fine-tune the shift

The Race of the Fallen Leaves

Sean Kelly

The Giro di Lombardia (Tour of Lombardy) is the last "Classic" of the professional road racing season. Nicknamed the "race of the fallen leaves," the race winds its way through the mountains surrounding Lake Cuomo in Northern Italy, a region of breathtaking scenic beauty. The race is a last flourish of professional road racing, before the long winter sees riders switch teams, retire or lose their form. For one last day, racers battle each other on steep climbs, descend at high speeds through stone-walled orchards, and race through medieval villages.

Irishman Sean Kelly knew the Giro di Lombardia well. He had launched his European cycling career by winning the amateur version of the event in 1976. His breakthrough as a professional came during the 1983 Giro di Lombardia, which he won against some of the best racers of the day. Over the next 8 years, Kelly became known as a dominant sprinter, winning the Tour de France's green jersey no less than four times. Unlike most sprinters, he was a well-rounded rider, equally at home on mountain stages in the great tours, on the cobbles of Paris-Roubaix, and in the break-aways of the Italian one-day Classics. Kelly won races from the season-opening Paris-Nice all the way to the Giro di Lombardia. His total of 193 professional victories is second only to the great Eddy Merckx.

By 1991, Kelly was 35 years old. Some considered him past his prime. In March, he had broken his collarbone. In July, his entire PDM team had pulled out of the Tour de France with a mysterious illness. As the leaves turned colors on the mountains above Lake Cuomo in October, Kelly had not yet won an important race.

The Giro di Lombardia was Kelly's last chance to prove his worth that year. Together with six other riders, he broke away on one of the steepest climbs. With Kelly's PDM teammates blocking at the front of the peloton, the breakaway quickly gained time. On the last ascent, Kelly and Martial Gayant went clear of their companions and raced toward the finish together. Even though Kelly did most of the work in the break, his superior sprint made the finish a foregone conclusion, and Kelly added a third victory at the Giro di Lombardia to his palmarès.

As autumn winds swept along the shores of Lake Cuomo, and the tourist hotels closed their shutters for the winter, Sean Kelly's incredible career continued to wind down as well. He won one more Classic before retiring.

▼ Sean Kelly was one of the last riders in the professional peloton to use toeclips and straps. Here he is riding in the 1991 Tour de France. (Photo: John Pierce/PhotoSport International)

Kelly's bike uses a traditional steel racing frame, equipped with Campagnolo's C-Record components. Introduced as an aerodynamic group to rival Shimano's Dura-Ace AX (p. 140), many racers found the new C-Record components heavier and less reliable than their predecessors, the classic Super Record. Kelly apparently agreed: His bike was equipped with Super Record pedals, and instead of the controversial "Delta" brakes, Kelly used the lighter and more powerful calipers from the cheaper Chorus group. One brake caliper fits inside the other, forked caliper for a more even force distribution.

In 1985, Shimano abandoned the aerodynamic concept and introduced indexed shifting, leaving Campagnolo trying to catch up. Catch up they did: After their first indexed "Syncro" shift levers were unsuccessful, Campagnolo finally copied Shimano's dual pivot, slant parallelogram rear derailleur in 1991. Kelly's bike used the new system, which worked very well. With these components, Campagnolo regained their leadership position among the makers of racing bicycle components.

A Classic Bike for the Hour Record

Tony Rominger

Tony Rominger was one of the greatest racers of the early 1990s, but his career was overshadowed by that of Miguel Indurain. Indurain used his superior time trialing skills to win five consecutive Tours de France and two Giri d'Italia. Rominger was the only one to challenge Indurain's superiority, and his memorable rides in the mountains during the 1993 Tour de France kept the outcome of the race wide open until the very end. Indurain prevailed, and Rominger finished in second place, less than 5 minutes behind.

With his great time trialing ability, Indurain seemed a natural for the hour record. In September 1994, he became the first cyclist to ride more than 53 km in an hour on his high-tech carbon-fiber Pinarello bicycle.

To everybody's surprise, Indurain's rival Tony Rominger went to the same velodrome in Bordeaux to attack the hour a few weeks after Indurain's record ride. The lightweight Rominger was known for his climbing more than for his ultimate power output, and he had no experience on the track at all. His hour record bike, built by Ernesto Colnago, was built along the lines of his time trial bike for the road. Rominger's first ride on the track did not start well. After only 60 meters, he entered the banked turn too slowly. His wheels slipped on the smooth track, and he crashed ignominiously. However, after two days of practicing his track riding skills, Tony Rominger felt ready to attack the hour record on October 22, 1994. And attack he did, improving on Indurain's record by a full 800 meters. Even so, he was remarkably fresh at the end of his record.

◀ Rominger at speed during his first hour record ride.
(Photo: Didier Mossiat, Photonews)

The bike shown here is his record bicycle. Unlike Francesco Moser's outlandish machine (see p. 152), Rominger's Colnago is a classic track bike, made from steel tubing. Fork blades as well as down and seat tubes are shaped as airfoils, and lenticular disc wheels reduce the aerodynamic resistance. More importantly, the aerodynamic handlebars enabled Rominger to adopt a very streamlined position, which greatly reduced the rider's wind resistance.

After this success, Colnago built a slightly refined bike along similar lines. Just a few weeks after his initial record attempt, Rominger returned to the Bordeaux velodrome for another run. This time, he gave it all he had, and improved his performance to an incredible 55.291 km. The following year, Indurain took his carbon fiber bike to the rarefied elevation of Colombia, but he was unable to match Rominger's performance. In fact, only one rider ever has gone faster than Rominger. Chris Boardman set a record of more than 56 km in 1996. Then the Union Cycliste Internationale (UCI) ruled that only traditional bikes with spoked wheels and standard drop bars could be used for hour records.

Rominger's position on the bike may not have qualified as traditional, but his bike showed that traditional frame-building techniques still are more than competitive in the age of carbon fiber.

Originality

Where possible, this book shows original bicycles that actually have served in competition. In a few cases, where original bikes do not exist for the type of competition I wanted to showcase, I included restored machines.

The original bikes, with original paint and components, in some cases even original tires, are not in pristine condition. Their patina is part of their history. Many of these bikes have led a hard life. Some parts have been changed as they wore out. As part of the specifications for each bike, we list parts that are not original, as far as we know.

 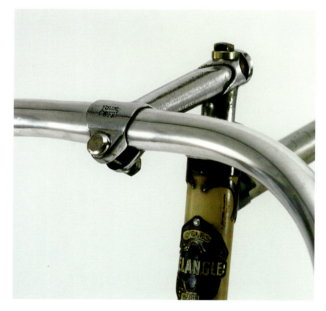

Specifications

The bicycles in this book illustrate the history of competition bicycles from the earliest days through the mid-1990s. Bicycles developed over time. Road surfaces changed, and so did tire sizes. Shorter races led to faster average speeds. New team tactics required different handling in high-speed sprints. Frame geometries adapted to these new conditions.

The following geometry drawings allow a comparison of the frames' angles and measurements, also in relation to handlebar widths and tire sizes. All measurements are in millimeters, center-to-center. Due to the difficulty of measuring bicycles without disassembly, the measurements are approximate (± 8 mm; ± 0.5°; ± 0.3 kg).

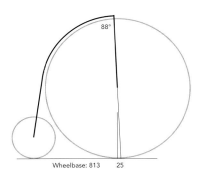

1880/85 Cycles Barret
Wheels: Front: 1400 mm; Rear: 420 mm, 16.5 mm solid rubber tires
Handlebar width: 680 mm
Crank length: 115-135 mm (adjustable)
Weight: 11.7 kg (25.8 lb.)

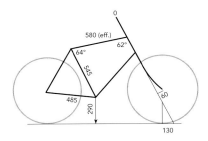

1894/95 Humber
Wheels: Front: 775 x 43 mm; Rear: 720 x 43 mm; clincher tires
Handlebar width: 555 mm
Crank length: 167.5 mm. Gearing: 18 x 8
Weight: 12.5 kg (27.5 lb.)

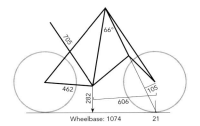

Ca. 1903 Dursley Pedersen
Wheels: 600 mm
Handlebar width: 460 mm
Crank length: 180 mm. Crank width (tread): 130 mm
Gearing: 28 x 8
Weight: 9.8 kg (21.6 lb.)

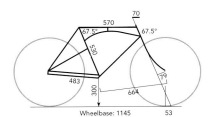

Ca. 1910 Labor Tour de France
Handlebar width: 383 mm
Crank length: 170 mm
Gearing: 48 x 18
Weight: 13.3 kg (29.3 lb.)
Non-original parts: Frame has been repainted

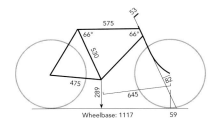

1926 Automoto Tour de France
Wheels: 700 mm
Handlebar width: 450 mm
Crank length: 167.5 mm
Gearing: 46 x 16 (fixed); 46 x 20 (freewheel)
Weight: 12.5 kg (27.6 lb.)

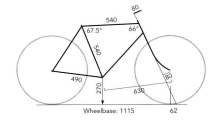

1927 Alcyon Tour de France
Wheels: 700 x 30 mm
Handlebar width: 465 mm
Crank length: 165 mm. Crank width (tread): 124 mm
Weight: 13.0 kg (28.7 lb.)
Non-original parts: AVA C45 aluminum rims (?)

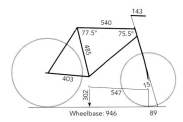

1920s Bastide Stayer
Handlebar width: 440 mm
Crank length: 170 mm
Weight: 9.6 kg (21.2 lb.)
Non-original parts: FB hubs, stem (?)

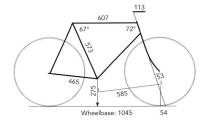

1930 Willy Appelhans 6-Day (F. Bartell)
Wheels: 700C tubulars
Crank length: 165 mm
Gearing: 40 x 8
Weight: 12.0 kg (26.5 lb.)
Non-original parts: Chainring is a replica.

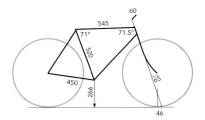

1935 Joe Kopsky (D. Kopsky)
Wheels: 700C tubulars
Weight: 9.1 kg (20.0 lb.)

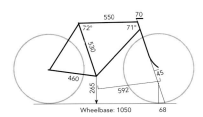

1939 Oscar Egg
Wheels: 700C tubulars
Handlebar width: 420 mm. Crank length: 165 mm
Gearing: 46 x 18-20 (freewheel); 46 x 17 (fixed)
Weight: 9.9 kg (21.8 lb.)
Non-original parts: Tires are narrower than original.

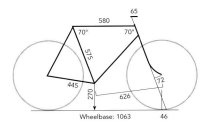

Ca. 1939 Caminargent Bordeaux-Paris
Wheels: 700C tubulars
Handlebar width: 390 mm
Crank length: 175 mm
Weight: 9.0 kg (19.8 lb.)
Non-original parts: tires, pedals

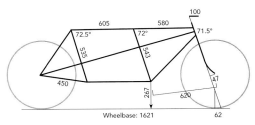

Ca. 1936 Delangle Tandem (M. Richard)
Wheels: 700C tubulars
Crank length: 170 mm
Weight: 16.5 kg (36.4 lb.)
Non-original parts: pedals, handlebars, saddles

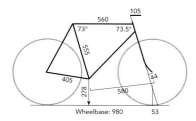

1939/1940 Delangle Track
Serial No.: 24237. Wheels: 700C tubulars
Handlebar width: 395 mm
Crank length: 170 mm
Weight: 8.1 kg (17.9 lb.)
Non-original parts: "Fausto Coppi" stem (?)

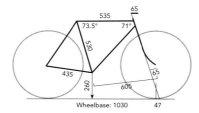

1948 Barralumin (R. Vietto)
Serial No.: 4074. Wheels: 700C tubulars
Crank length: 167.5 mm
Gearing: 48-44 x 14-22 (4-speed)
Weight: 8.0 kg (17.6 lb.) with pump
Non-original parts: handlebars, stem, tires, saddle (?).

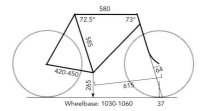

1948 Wilier Triestina (F. Magni)
Wheels: 700C tubulars
Handlebar width: 400 mm
Crank length: 172.5 mm
Weight: 10.5 kg (23.1 lb.)
Non-original parts: seatpost

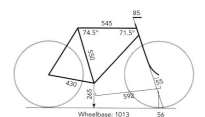

1949 Bartali (G. Bartali)
Serial No.: 49-04
Wheels: 700C tubulars
Handlebar width: 390 mm
Crank length: 167.5 mm
Weight: 10.5 kg (23.1 lb.)

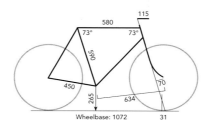

1949 Bianchi (F. Coppi)
Serial No.: 171 680. Wheels: 700C tubulars
Handlebar width: 400 mm. Crank length: 170 mm
Weight: 10.0 kg (22.0 lb.)
Non-original parts: For the 1949 Tour de France, the bike
was equipped with two chainrings and a front derailleur.

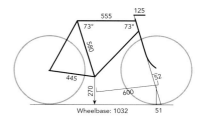

1951 René Herse Criterium des Porteurs
Wheels: 700C x 30 mm clinchers
Gearing: 48 x 18 (freewheel)
Weight: 11.6 kg (25.5 lb.)
Bike was recreated based on an original 1951 Herse frame
and an original Herse rack from a porteur racing bike.

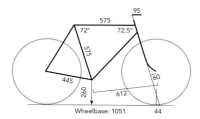

Ca. 1955 Bianco Road (Baudin)
Wheels: 700C tubulars
Handlebar width: 400 mm
Crank length: 170 mm
Crank width (tread): 129 mm
Weight: 10.8 kg (23.8 lb.)

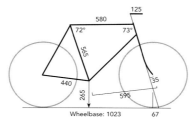

1950s Biancho Track (Baudin)
Wheels: 700C tubulars
Handlebar width: 400 mm
Crank length: 172.5 mm
Weight: 9.0 kg (19.8 lb.)
Non-original parts: pedals

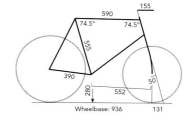

1930s Bastide Stayer (Baudin)
Wheels: Front: 570 mm; Rear: 700 mm tubulars
Crank length: 165 mm. Gearing: 30 x 7
Weight: 10.0 kg (22.0 lb.)
Non-original parts: The bike was repainted in the 1950s to
match Baudin's other bikes.

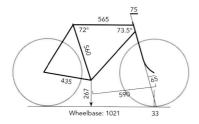

1950s Rochet Super Special
Wheels: 700C tubulars
Crank length: 170 mm
Handlebar width: 380 mm
Weight: 10.2 kg (22.5 lb.)

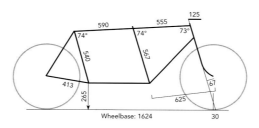

1948 René Herse Tandem (Détée/Bulté)
Serial No.: 201
Wheels: 650B x 35 mm clinchers
Crank length: Front: 170 mm; Rear: 165 mm
Weight: 18.2 kg (40.1 lb.)
Non-original parts: The tandem was completely restored to
its 1956 condition. Hubs have larger Alex Singer flanges.
Tubing decal on the fork is a later model. Rims; tires.

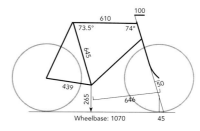

1965 Cinelli Supercorsa (B. Waddell)
Serial No.: 1626
Wheels: 700C x 23 mm tubulars
Handlebar width: 385 mm. Crank length: 170 mm
Crank width (tread): 134 mm
Gearing: 51-47 x 14-28 (5-speed)
Weight: 11.5 kg (25.3 lb.)

Specifications

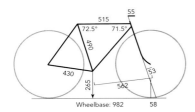

1970 René Herse Course (G. Gambillon)
Serial No.: 10 70. Wheels: 700C tubulars
Handlebar width: 385 mm
Crank length: 170 mm. Crank width: 135 mm
Weight: 9.6 kg (21.2 lb.)
Non-original parts: wheels (from another Herse team bike); toestraps.
For the 1972 world championships, the bike was equipped with
Campagnolo hubs and Huret Jubilee derailleurs.

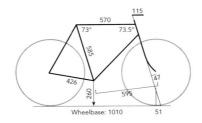

1974 Eddy Merckx/De Rosa (E. Merckx)
Wheels: 700C tubulars
Handlebar width: 425 mm
Crank length: 175 mm
Weight: 11.0 kg (24.3 lb.)
Non-original parts: wheels (?)

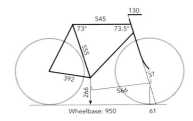

1975 Witcomb/J. P. Weigle (P. Weigle)
Wheels: 700C x 21.5 mm tubulars
Handlebar width: 405 mm
Weight: 8.3 kg (18.3 lb.)
Non-original parts: bottom bracket

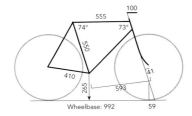

1981 Gitane (G. LeMond)
Serial No.: 7 1 - 81. Wheels: 700C x 21.5 mm tubulars
Handlebar width: 410 mm
Crank length: 172.5 mm. Crank width: 136 mm
Weight: 10.0 kg (22.0 lb.)
Non-original parts: Waterbottle is a contemporary
Specialized reproduction.

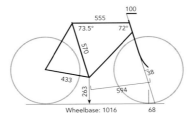

1982 Huffy/Mike Melton (J. Marino)
Wheels: 700C x 21 mm tubulars
Handlebar width: 415 mm
Crank length: 170 mm
Crank width (tread): 137 mm
Weight: 10.2 kg (22.5 lb.)

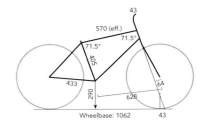

1983 Cunningham MTB (J. Phelan)
Wheels: 26" clinchers
Crank length: 175 mm
Weight: 11.9 kg (26.3 lb.)

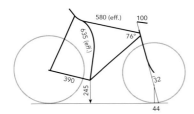

1983 Moser (F. Moser)
Wheels: Front: 650C; Rear: 720 mm tubulars
Handlebar width: 395 mm. Crank length: 170 mm
Weight: 9.0 kg (19.8 lb.)
Non-original parts: The gearing is different from that used in
the hour record. The bike is equipped with a 700C wheel.

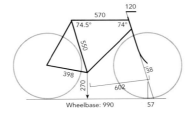

1988 Huffy/Landshark (A. Hampsten)
Wheels: 700C x 21.5 mm tubulars
Handlebar width: 415 mm
Crank length: 172.5 mm. Crank width (tread): 138 mm
Weight: 10.0 kg (22.0 lb.)
Non-original parts: wheels

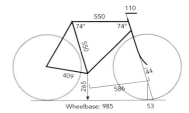

1991 Concorde (S. Kelly)
Serial No.: X910
Wheels: 700C x 21.5 mm tubulars
Handlebar width: 420 mm
Crank length: 172.5 mm. Crank width (tread): 143 mm
Weight: 10.3 kg (22.8 lb.)

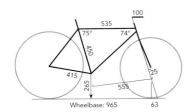

1994 Colnago (T. Rominger)
Wheels: Front: 650C; Rear: 700C tubulars
Crank length: 172.5 mm
Weight: 7.5 kg (16.5 lb.)
Non-original parts: The gearing is different from that used
in the hour record.

Authenticity

I knew it would be a difficult task to find the actual bikes of the great champions for this book, because there are so many misrepresented bikes and outright fakes. It appears that nearly every early 1950s Bianchi in a frame size of roughly 59 cm now claims to have been one of Fausto Coppi's bikes.

The author and numerous contributors have established the authenticity of the bikes shown in these pages to the best of their knowledge. In some cases, it is impossible to prove that the bikes were ridden by the famous racers in specific events. In most cases, the authenticity comes through the history of the bikes, which were purchased from the racers themselves or donated by them to museums.

We rejected many bikes, even after we had photographed them, either because our research showed them to be obvious fakes, or because we could not authenticate them beyond reasonable doubt. In some cases (E. Merckx, A. Hampsten, F. Moser), there are two identical bikes, one ridden in the event, the other a backup. It is difficult to establish decades after the fact which is which. And one bike (p. 94) is a recreation of an extinct breed. Overall, I am confident that most bikes in these pages are what they purport to be.

G. LeMond's Gitane

G. Bartali's Bartali

G. Gambillon's René Herse

S. Kelly's Concorde

G. LeMond's Gitane/S. Kelly's Concorde

J. Phelan's Cunningham

THE AUTHOR
Jan Heine is the editor of *Bicycle Quarterly*, a magazine about classic bicycles, cycling history and bicycle technology. Jan raced for ten years. Today, he prefers randonneuring and long-distance cycling. He loves cycling with his family in his hometown of Seattle.

◂ Jan racing in 1995.

THE PHOTOGRAPHER
Jean-Pierre Pradères is a free-lance photograper specializing in motorcycle and bicycle subjects. His photographs have been published in the Guggenheim Museum's *The Art of the Motorcycle*, in Vintage Bicycle Press' *The Golden Age of Handbuilt Bicycles* and in numerous magazines.

THE GRAPHIC DESIGNER
Christophe Courbou is a freelance graphic designer. For 4 years, he raced bicycles as an amateur in France. Today, he prefers cyclotouring in the Massif Central of France, where he lives with his family at the top of a 5 km, 8% climb.

◂ Christophe racing in 1989.

CONTRIBUTORS

The bikes shown in these pages were loaned for photography by their generous owners:

- Cappella della Madonna del Ghisallo, Italy
- Jeff Groman (Classic Cycle, Bainbridge Island, WA)
- Andy Hampsten (Hampsten Cycles)
- Raymond Henry
- Chris Kostman (AdventureCorps)
- Jean Lalan
- Fiorenzo Magni
- Helen March
- Museo del Ciclismo, Magreglio, Italy
- Jacquie Phelan
- Vance Sprock (Cupertino Bicycle Shop)
- Peter Weigle (J. P. Weigle Cycles)

Many others have assisted in the preparation of this book. They went out of their way to make sure that the bikes were available for photography. They helped with historic photos and research. They reviewed the final text. We greatly appreciate their enthusiasm and help.

Gordon Bainbridge, Gilbert Bulté, Eowyn Ceruti, Danièle Crueize, Ernest & Olivier Csuka (Cycles Alex Singer), Lucien Détée, Ken Dobb, Marc Elliott (Color Services), Glenn Erickson, David Evans, Geneviève Gambillon, George Gibbs (Il Vecchio Bicycles), Curt Goodrich, Charles Hadrann (Wright Bros Cycle Works), Stephen Hampsten (Hampsten Cycles), Lyli Herse, Ken Johnson, Mike Kone (René Herse Bicycles), Claudine Lalan, Jack Liskear (En Selle Bicycles), Alexander & Neville March, Don Meth (Show Quality Metal Finishing), Joel Metz, Nelson Miller, Peter Miller (Peter Miller Books), Ted Mock, Ronan Morel, Mark Petry, John Pierce (Photosport International), Jeff Potter (OYB Press), Gary Prangle (Screen Specalties), Daniel Provot, Mads Rasmussen, Bill Rehberg (Shadowflight), Claude Reynaud (Musée Moto-Vélo), Aldo Ross, Hahn Rossman (Alki Foundry), Dietrich Schmidt, Jacques Seray, Lorne Shields, John Slawta (Landshark Bicycles), Eric Svoboda, Hervé Thomas, Elliot Toler-Scott (El-Hot Metal Fabrications), Donn Trethewey, Mark Vande Kamp, Bruce Waddell, Alex Wetmore.

Copyright ©2008 Vintage Bicycle Press
All Rights Reserved

First Edition

Published by Vintage Bicycle Press
140 Lakeside Ave., Ste. C • Seattle WA 98122 • USA
www.vintagebicyclepress.com

Printed in Singapore by CS Graphics

Cover photo: Eddy Merckx' bike from the 1974 World Championships

Publisher's cataloging in Publication Data
Heine, Jan, 1968-
The Competition Bicycle – A Photographic History. First Edition.
p: 176. 30.0 cm. Includes bibliographic information
1. Bicycles and bicycling
2. History of technology
3. Sports
I. Authorship
II. Title: The Competition Bicycle – A Photographic History.
ISBN 978-0-9765460-1-6 (hardcover)
Library of Congress Control Number 2008936365